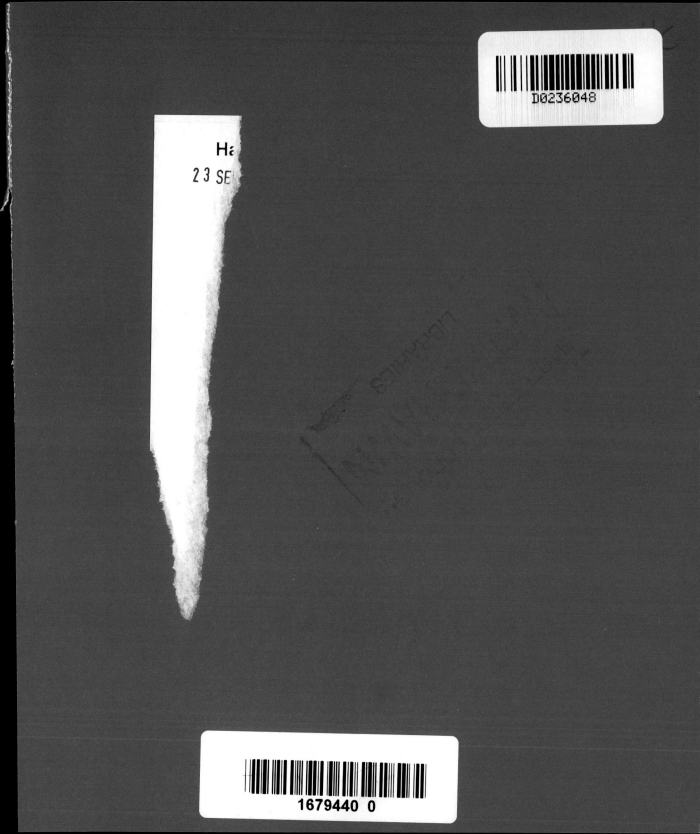

Writing Stories
Scary Stories

Anita Ganeri

Raintree is an imprint of Capstone Global Library Limited, a company incorporated in England and Wales having its registered office at 7 Pilgrim Street, London, EC4V 6LB – Registered company number: 6695582

To contact Raintree:
Phone: 0845 6044371
Fax: + 44 (0) 1865 312263
Email: myorders@raintreepublishers.co.uk
Outside the UK please telephone +44 1865 312262.

Text © Capstone Global Library Limited 2013
First published in hardback in 2013
The moral rights of the proprietor have been asserted.

Edited by Dan Nunn, Rebecca Rissman, and Sian Smith
Designed by Joanna Hinton-Malivoire
Original illustrations © Capstone Global Library 2013
Picture research by Ruth Blair
Production by Sophia Argyris
Originated by Capstone Global Library Ltd
Printed and bound in China by South China Printing Company Ltd

ISBN 978 1 406 26039 7
17 16 15 14 13
10 9 8 7 6 5 4 3 2 1

British Library Cataloguing in Publication Data
Ganeri, Anita, 1961-
 Scary stories. -- (Writing stories) 1. Horror tales--Authorship--Juvenile literature. 2. Ghost stories--Authorship--Juvenile literature. 3. Horror tales. 4. Children's stories.
I. Title II. Series
  808.3'873-dc23

Acknowledgements
We would like to thank the following for permission to reproduce photographs: Alamy p.5 (© tony french); Corbis p.7 (© Bettmann); Shutterstock background images and design features, pp.4 (© SergiyN), 6 (© dragon_fang), 8 (© CREATISTA), 9 (© Kamira), 12 (© Linda Bucklin), 14 (© Devid Camerlynck), 16 (© Monkey Business Images), 18 (© Ensuper), 20 (© Monkey Business Images), 22 (© Estremo), 24 (© Nomad_Soul), 26 (© doglikehorse)

Cover photographs reproduced with permission of Shutterstock: spooky tree (© Nejron Photo), background (© prudkov).

Every effort has been made to contact copyright holders of material reproduced in this book. Any omissions will be rectified in subsequent printings if notice is given to the publisher.

Some words are shown in bold, **like this**. You can find out what they mean by looking in the glossary.

Contents

Follow this symbol to read a scary story.

What is a story?

A story is a piece of **fiction** writing. It tells the reader about made-up people, places, and events. A story needs a **setting**, **characters**, and a **plot**. You should try to work these out before you start writing.

There are lots of different types of stories. You can write mystery stories, silly stories, fairy tales, adventure stories, animal stories, and lots more. This book is about writing scary stories.

Scary stories

A scary story should have spooky **characters** and a scary **setting**, such as a haunted house or castle. It should be exciting and scary at the same time.

A Christmas Carol by Charles Dickens is a famous scary story. It tells the tale of a very mean man, called Scrooge, who is haunted by the ghosts of Christmas past, present, and future. In the end, Scrooge becomes much kinder and more generous.

Collecting ideas

You can get ideas for writing your own scary story from books, the internet, TV, or from your imagination. It is also good to read scary stories by other writers. This can spark off ideas and help you to make your own writing better.

Quickly write any ideas you have down in a notebook so that you do not forget them. Then you can go back to them later. Keep the notebook handy at all times, even by your bed. You never know when a brilliant idea will come.

Plot planning

Before you start writing, you need to plan your **plot**. This means what happens in your story. The plot needs a beginning, a middle, and an end. You can try using a **story mountain** to help you.

Middle
The main action happens. There may be a problem for one of your characters.

Beginning
Set the scene and introduce your main **characters**.

Ending
The problem is solved and the story ends.

Your story starts at one side of the mountain, goes up to the top, then down the other side.

You could also try marking the main events on a **timeline**. This will help you to put them in the right order. Here is a timeline for the scary story in this book.

Children on holiday see an old house.

A boy tells them that the house is haunted.

They say that they don't believe in ghosts.

The boy takes them to the house.

Inside the house, they hear spooky noises.

Then they see a ghostly figure.

They run away from the house.

They are sure they know who the ghost is.

Starting your story

Your story needs a strong beginning that grabs your readers' attention. It should make them want to keep reading. It is also a good place to introduce your main **characters**.

Sam looked up at the rambling old house on the hill and shivered.

Give your story a scary start.

A Spooky Story

Sam looked up at the rambling old house on the hill and shivered.

Daisy followed his gaze. It was the first day of the children's summer holiday. While their parents were inside unpacking, the twins had gone into the garden to explore.

Spooky settings

Setting the scene means deciding on the place and time in which your story is set. It tells your reader where and when the story happens. It brings your story to life. An old, creepy house, like the one below, is a great **setting** for a scary story.

The children couldn't stop looking at the creepy house. It was crumbling and covered in ivy. It had broken windows and a big wooden door. It looked old and gloomy, and it creaked in the wind. Daisy thought that it was the spookiest place she had ever seen.

 Describe what your setting looks and sounds like.

Character building

Create strong and interesting **characters** for your story. Keep fact files, like the ones below, for the main characters. Think about what they look like and about their thoughts and feelings.

Character fact file
Characters: Sam and Daisy (twins)
Age: about 8
Look like: short, dark hair
Personalities: curious; very daring
Like: going on holiday; having adventures
Dislike: green vegetables; having to go to bed

Character fact file
Character: Mysterious boy
Age: unknown
Looks like: small; pale-skinned
Personality: quiet; sad; far-away look
Likes: telling stories
Dislikes: not being believed

The twins and the mysterious boy are the main characters in our story.

Suddenly, a boy appeared next to them. Sam and Daisy jumped.

"It's haunted," the boy said, pointing at the house. "A hundred years ago, a boy who lived there died in a terrible accident. Today, his ghost haunts the house."

There was something strange about the boy, the twins thought. He was very pale, and he looked very sad.

Try drawing pictures of your characters to help you work out what they are like.

In the middle

The middle of your story is where the main action happens. You might have several ideas for how your story will work out. Use a **story map**, like the one below, to help you decide which idea will work best.

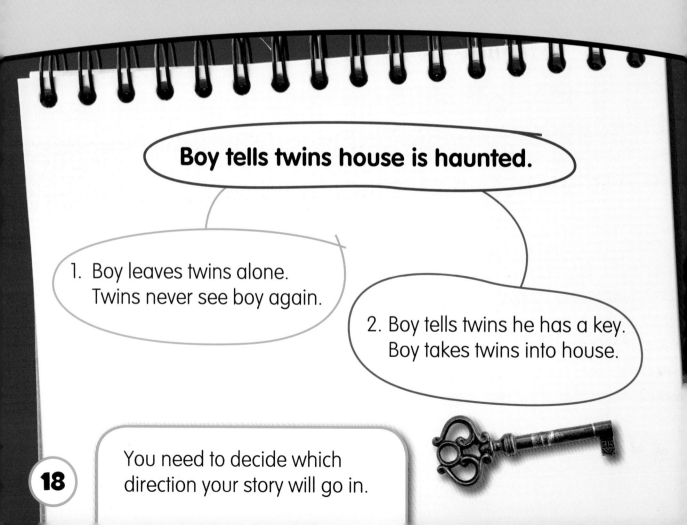

Boy tells twins house is haunted.

1. Boy leaves twins alone. Twins never see boy again.

2. Boy tells twins he has a key. Boy takes twins into house.

You need to decide which direction your story will go in.

"We don't believe in ghosts," said Sam and Daisy, together.

The boy shrugged. He told the twins that he would prove it. He had a key to the house and could let them in.

"Okay," said Daisy, bravely. "But we'll have to be quick. Our parents will be looking for us."

Speaking parts

Dialogue means the words people say. You can use it in your story to bring your **characters** to life and make them more believable. It is also a useful way of bringing your readers into the action.

"What's that?" said Sam, as they stood in the dusty hallway. "I'm sure I heard a noise."

Put **speech marks** around the spoken words.

"What's that?" said Sam, as they stood in the dusty hallway. "I'm sure I heard a noise."

"I heard it, too," said Daisy. "It sounded like someone crying."

The boy said nothing. He just sighed sadly.

"It seems to be getting closer," whispered Sam.

"Yikes!" squeaked Daisy. "It's a..."

Dialogue can make your writing more **dramatic** and exciting.

What happens next?

The middle of your story is also where your **characters** face a problem or there is a **dramatic** event. Here are some dramatic events that could happen in your scary story. Can you think of any more?

- Twins see a ghost.
- Boy vanishes without a trace.
- House owner appears.
- Twins are trapped inside the house.
- The house falls down.

Several things might happen at the same time.

"...ghost!"

In front of them stood the ghostly figure of a boy. He looked very sad. The twins stood still. They were too frightened to move. They looked round for the boy they had come with. But he was nowhere to be seen.

The middle of your story should keep your readers guessing.

Exciting writing

In a scary story, it is important to make your writing exciting. Choose your words carefully. For example, add lots of interesting **adjectives** to describe your **characters** and **setting**.

Useful adjectives

creepy

gloomy

hair-raising

terrified

ghostly

Can you think of any more?

Sam and Daisy were terrified. Alone in the creepy house, they trembled with fear. Where had the mysterious boy gone? What was the ghostly shape? They looked at each other. Then they ran out of the house as fast as they could.

 Can you pick out the adjectives on this page?

More top tips

1 A scary story should be exciting. Use short sentences or phrases to speed up the **pace** of your writing and add excitement.

2 Read your story out loud when you've finished it. This will help you to see if it flows well right up to the end.

3 Read your story through and correct any mistakes. You might need to do this several times before you are happy with it.

4 Do some research for your scary story by visiting a haunted house or castle. Don't forget your notebook for jotting down ideas.

5 Draw pictures of your **characters** and **setting**. This can help you to bring them to life and describe what they are like.

6 Don't give too much away early in your story. In a scary story, you want your reader to keep guessing right to the end.

Glossary

adjectives words that describe nouns (nouns are naming words)

characters people in a piece of writing

dialogue words that characters say

dramatic very exciting

fiction piece of writing that is about made-up places, events, and characters

pace speed at which a story moves along

plot what happens in a story

setting time and place in which a story is set

speech marks marks that show the words someone has spoken

story map diagram that helps you decide the next step of the plot

story mountain mountain-shaped diagram that helps you to plan out a story

timeline list of events in the order in which they happen

Find out more

Books

How to Write Stories, Celia Warren (QED Publishing, 2008)

Writing Stories, Anita Ganeri (Raintree Publishing, 2013)

Write Your Own Story Book, Louie Stowell and Jane Chisholm (Usborne Publishing, 2011)

Websites

www.bbc.co.uk/schools/ks2bitesize/english/writing

Learn how to improve your writing skills on this website.

www.readwritethink.org/files/resources/interactives/cube_creator/

The writing cubes on this website will help you to create your own stories.

Index